JANET RENO
First Woman Attorney General

Janet Reno

JANET RENO
First Woman Attorney General

By Charnan Simon

CHILDRENS PRESS ®
CHICAGO

PHOTO CREDITS

Courtesy of Department of Justice—cover
AP/Wide World—3, 29
The Miami Herald—5, 6, 7, 11, 13, 15, 19, 22, 25
The Palm Beach Post—2, 16, 17, 21, 26
Reuters/Bettmann—1, 30, 31, 32
© Marc Pesetsky/Silver Image—8

EDITORIAL STAFF

Project Editor: Mark Friedman
Design and Electric Composition: Biner Design
Photo Editor: Jan Izzo

Library of Congress Cataloging-in-Publication Data

Simon, Charnan.
    Janet Reno: first woman attorney general/by Charnan
Simon.
        p. cm. — (Picture story biography)
        ISBN 0-516-04191-6
        1. Reno, Janet, 1938—Juvenile literature. 2. Attorneys
general—United States—Biography—Juvenile literature.
[1. Reno, Janet, 1938- . 2. Attorneys general. 3.Women—
Biography.] I. Title. II. Series: Picture-story biographies.

KF373.R45S56 1994   93-42852
353.5'092—dc20   CIP
[B]   AC

WHEN JANET RENO was growing up, there was one rule her mother insisted she obey. Mrs. Reno didn't care much about the little things, like wiping your feet, or keeping your elbows off the table, or reading in bed with a flashlight. She did care about the "good, better, best" rule. This rule said, "Don't ever rest until good is better, and better is best."

Janet and her mother in front of the family house

Janet Reno must have been thinking about her mother's rule on March 12, 1993. That was the day she became the seventy-eighth attorney general of the United States. She was the first woman to be named the country's top law enforcer.

As she accepted her new job, Janet Reno promised to uphold the laws of the United States and see that justice was carried out in the land. Everyone who heard her knew she would do her best.

Janet Reno was born in Miami, Florida, on July 21, 1938. Her parents, Henry and Jane Reno, were both

Janet's father, Henry Reno

A very young Janet Reno

newspaper reporters. Although the Renos worked in the city, they wanted to raise their children in the country. So when Janet was eight years old, the family moved 20 miles outside of Miami. They lived on 21 acres of wilderness near the Florida Everglades.

Even though they lived out in the country, Janet's parents still worked. Her father went to work in Miami every day, and her mother wrote articles from their house. At the same time, her mother was building the house!

Janet described how her mother built their home: "She dug the foundation with a pick and shovel, she laid the brick, she put in the plumbing, and my father would help her with heavy work at night."

The house that Janet's mother built

Sometimes the children also helped build the house. "Unload the rest of the bricks from the jeep," their mother would say, "and then you can ride the pony."

The Reno house is still standing, more than forty years later. Not even Hurricane Andrew could do worse than knock a few shingles off the roof. When she is not in Washington, D.C., carrying out her duties as attorney general, this is still Janet Reno's home.

"I have lived there ever since [childhood]," Reno happily says. "And as I come down the driveway through the woods with a new problem to solve, that house stands as a symbol to me, that you can do anything you really want to, if it's the right thing to do and you put your mind to it."

The house had no air conditioning, no washer or dryer, and no television—

Janet's mother said that television led to "mind rot." Instead of watching TV, Janet and her two brothers and one sister invented their own fun. They canoed and camped and hiked through the woods. They played baseball and rode ponies, and took care of the family animals—donkeys, goats, cows, and a flock of peacocks (all named Horace!). When the weather was bad, they came inside to read and play Scrabble and argue and laugh.

Janet was interested in just about everything as a girl. She wanted to be a major league baseball pitcher when she grew up. But she changed her mind often—she also wanted to be a doctor, a rancher, a marine biologist, and a foreign service officer. When she finally decided to become a lawyer, she said it was because "I didn't want anyone telling me what to do!"

As a teenager, Janet loved rugged country life.

Becoming a lawyer is not easy. Lawyers go to school for many years to learn our nation's laws. A lawyer has to think clearly and must enjoy solving difficult problems. She must read a lot, and remember what she reads. She must be able to speak and write clearly.

Some lawyers work in courtrooms. Others work for large corporations, or for a single person (the people or companies that hire lawyers are called clients). No matter where she works, a lawyer's main job is to help her clients understand what the law will or will not allow them to do. She must at all times explain and protect her clients' rights.

Janet Reno began preparing to be a lawyer even before she was sure she wanted to be one. She was a debating champion at Coral Gables High School. This taught her how to argue a case and

convince a judge that she was right.
When Janet spoke, people listened!

In college, Janet continued to
develop as a strong leader. She majored
in chemistry at Cornell University,
where she was also the president of the
Women's Student Government.

On a trip home from college, Janet's proud parents meet her at the airport.

Janet's 1960 Harvard Law School yearbook photo

Finally, in 1960, Janet Reno enrolled in Harvard Law School. Out of more than five hundred students, she was one of only sixteen women who finished the program and graduated. Like her mother before her, Janet Reno proved that she could do anything she wanted, if she just put her mind to it.

Not everything came easily to Janet. When she first graduated from law school, she had trouble finding a job. One large law firm in Miami wouldn't hire her because she was a woman. She refused to be discouraged. She promptly found another job with a smaller firm. Four years later, she was named a junior partner in the law firm of Lewis and Reno.

Janet got her first taste of politics in 1971. She was appointed the staff director of the Judiciary Committee of

After much effort, Janet finally found a job as a lawyer.

the Florida House of Representatives. Her work on this committee helped to completely reorganize the Florida court system.

Reno liked the world of politics. The following year, in 1972, she ran for a seat in the Florida state legislature. To her great disappointment, she lost the

In the early 1970s, Janet began working in politics. Here she debates Boca Raton Mayor William Miller (right).

Janet as a candidate for the Florida House of Representatives in 1972

election. Once again, she refused to be discouraged. Instead, she comforted herself by reading a biography of Abraham Lincoln, who was also a lawyer until he entered politics. "He's a man I greatly admire," Reno said. "And I was cheered to learn that he had lost his first election."

Just because she lost an election did not mean that Janet Reno was finished with politics. In 1973, she worked on the state senate's Criminal Justice Committee. This time, instead of reorganizing Florida's courts, she helped reorganize their criminal code—the rules by which suspected criminals are tried for their crimes.

Later that same year, Reno was hired by Richard Gerstein, a Florida state attorney. ("Attorney" is another name for "lawyer.") Gerstein told her to organize a juvenile department for young people who had been arrested. He probably didn't expect much from her because other lawyers had tried organizing the juvenile system, but they had all failed. Once again, Janet Reno proved her worth. Gerstein later said, "I figured she would dawdle around like everybody else and write

A group of lawyers gather in Janet's office for a meeting.

another report. Instead, she pasted the juvenile court together in about two months."

Reno went back to working with her own clients after she left the state attorney's office in 1976. But Richard Gerstein didn't forget the bright and energetic young lawyer who had reorganized his juvenile court system. He wanted Janet Reno to replace him when he left the state attorney's office.

Usually, state attorneys are elected to office. But when Richard Gerstein retired in 1978, there were still several months left in his term. This meant that the governor of Florida had to appoint someone to act as state attorney until the next election.

Gerstein thought Janet Reno would be the perfect choice. The governor agreed. In 1978, he appointed Janet Reno as Dade County state attorney. She was the first woman ever to hold a state attorney post in the state of Florida.

Janet Reno knew she had a big job ahead of her. In the United States, people who are accused of committing crimes cannot simply be thrown in jail and kept there. They must first be

Janet is sworn in as Florida's new state attorney in 1978.

proven guilty in a court of law. Our legal system is set up this way to protect the rights of all U.S. citizens. The courts want to be sure that people don't get punished for things they really didn't do.

A state attorney takes the government's side in court cases. They are known as prosecutors because it is

21

State Attorney Reno argues a case in court.

their job to prosecute an accused
person, who is called the defendant.
The prosecutor must convince the
court that the defendant is guilty of the
crimes for which he or she was
arrested.

　　The accused person is defended in
court by a defense attorney. This
lawyer must convince the court that
the defendant is innocent of the crimes.

After listening to both the defense attorney and the prosecutor, a judge or a jury decides whether they think the accused is innocent or guilty. And even when someone is found guilty of a crime, he or she still has rights under the law that must be protected.

As Dade County state attorney, Janet Reno was the chief prosecutor in the largest law office in the entire state. She and her office handled more than 120,000 cases every year!

Miami was a city with many problems. Illegal immigrants often tried to enter Florida from nearby islands in the Caribbean. People of different races couldn't always get along in the city. Drug dealers and street gangs fought each other in deadly gun battles.

State Attorney Reno had her hands full trying to keep lawbreakers off Miami's streets. She and the lawyers working for her won some of their cases, and they lost some. Through it all, however, Reno earned a reputation for being a tough but fair prosecutor. As one city official said, "As state attorney, people aren't going to love you always, but she is definitely respected and seen as fair."

Janet Reno recognized that there was more to her job than just putting criminals in jail. She wanted people to learn to live honest lives out of jail. To do this, they needed education, housing, jobs, and counseling to help give up drug habits.

Reno believed in fighting crime at early ages. She was convinced that if all children had good homes, good schools, and good health care, they wouldn't want to grow up to break the law. She worked hard to steer

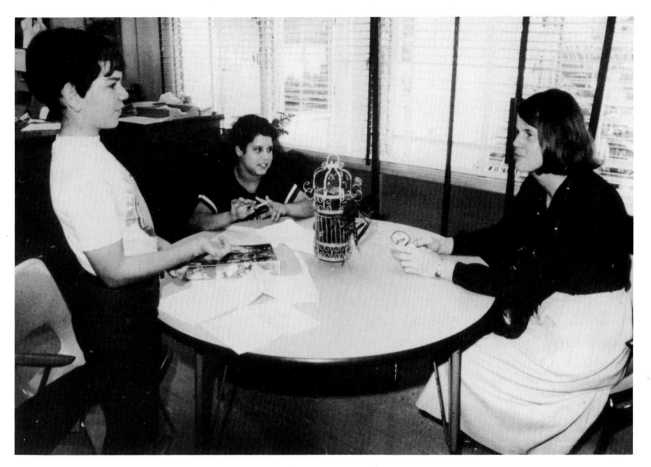

Janet talks to Florida schoolchildren to better understand their concerns.

young people away from crime, and to make Miami neighborhoods safe for everyone.

Still, Janet Reno could be tough on crime when she had to be. She demanded and won long prison

Janet appears at a press conference with Florida law enforcement officials.

sentences when she felt criminals
deserved them. "I want to let people
know that crime doesn't pay," she said
firmly.

Janet Reno's hard work paid off.
She was reelected as state attorney four
times. In the last election, nobody even
wanted to run against her, so she won
unchallenged!

Janet Reno's reputation as a respected law enforcer spread beyond Miami. When Bill Clinton was elected president in November 1992, one of his first jobs was to appoint a new attorney general. His staff asked Janet Reno if she was interested in the position. At the time, Janet's mother was dying of lung cancer. She was too busy nursing her mother to take on the responsibility of being the nation's top law enforcer. She turned down the president's request.

President Clinton went on to interview several other candidates for the job. He eventually chose a lawyer named Zoë Baird. When the president nominates a new cabinet member, the nominee is questioned by a Senate subcommittee. They look into the applicant's background and determine if he or she is qualified to serve on the cabinet. In January 1993, it looked like the Senate might not approve Baird's nomination. Several years before, she had employed a nanny and a driver and had not paid their taxes properly. She admitted she had broken the law, and the American public reacted negatively. In a storm of controversy, Zoë Baird withdrew her nomination in late January.

President Clinton needed a new candidate immediately—a qualified lawyer with a spotless record. He again turned to Janet Reno.

Reno's mother had died in December 1992, so she now felt she could live in Washington and devote her full attention to this important job. She didn't hesitate to accept the president's request. Her confirmation hearings with the Senate went smoothly and quickly. On March 12,

Janet's niece holds the bible as Supreme Court Justice Byron White administers the oath of office to the new attorney general.

1993, Janet Reno was sworn in as the first woman attorney general in United States history.

Attorney General Reno knows she will face many challenges as the head of our country's Justice Department. She is committed to fighting crime and to punishing criminals when they deserve it. But she is just as committed to fighting crime before it happens. She still believes that the best way to stop crime is to erase poverty, improve education and health care, and make sure there are enough jobs for everyone.

As attorney general, one of Janet's top priorities is the education and welfare of the nation's children.

Attorney General Reno lays it on the line at a press conference.

Becoming attorney general has not changed Janet Reno. She still likes hiking, camping, and canoeing in her beloved Everglades. When she can get away from Washington, D.C., she entertains her nieces and nephews in the old family home outside of Miami. And no matter how tough things get in the attorney general's office, she always tries to live up to her mother's motto: "Don't ever rest until good is better, and better is best."

JANET RENO

1938	July 21—Janet is born in Miami, Florida, to Henry and Jane Reno
1949	Jane Reno completes the family home near the Florida Everglades
1956	Enters Cornell University
1960	Enters Harvard Law School
1967	Henry Reno dies
1971	Works in the Florida House of Representatives
1972	Loses election to Florida state legislature
1973-1976	Works for Florida state attorney's office
1978	Named Dade County (FL) state attorney (is eventually reelected to the office four times)
1992	November—Turns down President-elect Clinton's invitation to be attorney general
1992	December—Jane Reno dies
1993	February—Accepts Clinton's second offer to be attorney general
1993	March 12—Sworn in as first woman attorney general in U.S. history

INDEX

ABOUT THE AUTHOR

Charnan Simon began her publishing career in the Children's Book Department of Little, Brown, and Company. After that she spent five busy years editing Cricket Magazine, where she read hundreds of great children's books and met many talented writers and artists. All of this was a tremendous help when she started writing her own books for young readers. Ms. Simon's most recent title for Childrens Press was *Midori: Brilliant Violinist*. She lives in Chicago with her husband and two daughters, and she enjoys reading—and writing—history, biography, and fiction of all sorts.